Celebrate Reading with us!

With A Crash And A BANG!

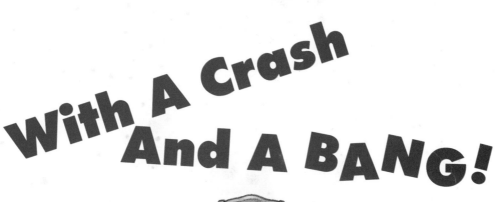

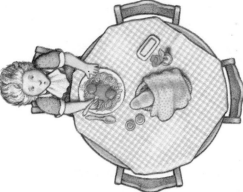

Senior Author
John J. Pikulski

*Senior Coordinating
Author*
J. David Cooper

*Senior Consulting
Author*
William K. Durr

Coordinating Authors
Kathryn H. Au
M. Jean Greenlaw
Marjorie Y. Lipson
Susan E. Page
Sheila W. Valencia
Karen K. Wixson

Authors
Rosalinda B. Barrera
Edwina Bradley
Ruth P. Bunyan
Jacqueline L. Chaparro
Jacqueline C. Comas
Alan N. Crawford
Robert L. Hillerich
Timothy G. Johnson
Jana M. Mason
Pamela A. Mason
William E. Nagy
Joseph S. Renzulli
Alfredo Schifini

Senior Advisor
Richard C. Anderson

Advisors
Christopher J. Baker
Charles Peters
MaryEllen Vogt

HOUGHTON MIFFLIN COMPANY   BOSTON
Atlanta   Dallas   Geneva, Illinois   Palo Alto   Princeton   Toronto

3

10

Surprise!

14

🎗 This Is the Bear   *by Sarah Hayes*

28

Surprising Riddles

31

🎗 Fix-It   *by David McPhail*

45

🎗 How to Hide a Polar Bear and
Other Mammals
by Ruth Heller

60

🎗 Do Like Kyla   *by Angela Johnson*

🎗 Award Winner

4

POETRY
30
Surprises
by Jean Conder Soule

43
✿ Drinking Fountain
by Marchette Chute

44
✿ This Tooth
by Lee Bennett Hopkins

📖

THEME BOOKS
✿ The Cake That Mack Ate
by Rose Robart
✿ Daddy Has a Pair of Striped Shorts
by Mimi Otey

80

Scared Silly

84

☆ Klippity Klop
by Ed Emberley

114

Chinese Dragons
an informational article

119

☆ The Gunnywolf
by A. Delaney

132

Monsters and Dragons   *a photo essay*

134

🎖 Strange Bumps
a story from Owl at Home
by Arnold Lobel

POETRY
118

A Long-haired Griggle
by Alice Gilbert

147

The Monster Stomp
by John Perry

THEME BOOKS
🎖 Monster Tracks?
by A. Delaney
🎖 I Am Scared   *by Ivar Da Coll*
translated from Spanish

THEME 3

150

CATS

154

No One Should Have Six Cats!
by Susan Mathias Smith

176

Tiger Runs   *by Derek Hall*

188

All Kinds of Cats   *a photo essay*

192

Chitina and Her Cat
by Montserrat del Amo
translated from Spanish

208

Cat's Out of the Bag
jokes by Sharon Friedman and Irene Shere

POETRY
174
✦ At Night   *by Aileen Fisher*
✦ Cats Sleep Anywhere   *by Eleanor Farjeon*

175
The House Cat   *by Annette Wynne*
Cat Kisses   *by Bobbi Katz*

186
Lion   *by N. M. Bodecker*

187
The Tiger   *by Ernesto Galarza*
translated from Spanish

THEME BOOKS
Charles Tiger   *by Siobhan Dodds*
✦ Young Lions   *by Toshi Yoshida*

READING SOCIAL STUDIES
212
Who Can Fix It?

GLOSSARY
218

Surprise!

You can find surprises everywhere — especially in books! These stories and poems may have some surprises for *you!*

CONTENTS

This Is the Bear   14
by Sarah Hayes
illustrated by Helen Craig

Fix-It   31
written and illustrated by David McPhail

How to Hide a Polar Bear and Other Mammals   45
written and illustrated by Ruth Heller

Do Like Kyla   60
by Angela Johnson
illustrated by James E. Ransome

THIS IS THE
BEAR

by Sarah Hayes
illustrated by Helen Craig

This is the bear
who fell in the bin.
This is the dog
who pushed him in.

This is the man
who picked up the sack.
This is the driver
who would not come back.

This is the bear
who went to the dump
and fell on the pile
with a bit of a bump.

Ouch!

This is the boy
who took the bus
and went to the dump
to make a fuss.

Find my bear!

You must be joking.

This is the man
in an awful grump
who searched
and searched
and searched the dump.

This is the bear
all cold and cross
who never thought
he was really lost.

Here I am.

This is the man
who drove them home —
the boy, the bear
and the dog with a bone.

This is the bear
neat as a pin
who would not say
just where he had been.

A little trip.

This is the boy
who knew quite well,
but promised his friend
he would not tell.

And this is the boy
who woke up in the night
and asked the bear
if he felt all right —
and was very surprised
when the bear gave a shout,
"How soon can we have
another day out?"

Another Day Out

Did the ending surprise you? Why do
you think the bear wanted another day out?
Think of some place the boy and the
bear might go together. Draw some pictures.
Then write about your ideas.

Meet the Author

Sarah Hayes has written many books for children. Some of her other books are *Eat Up, Gemma* and *Bad Egg: The Story of Humpty Dumpty*. She also reads many children's books and then writes about them for magazines. Her reviews of these books help children and parents decide which books they want to read.

Meet the Illustrator

Helen Craig has illustrated about twenty books. She says that before making final pictures for a book, she likes to practice. She practices by making tiny pictures of all of the pages. When she knows what pictures she wants to use, she practices making the same pictures larger. Then, she carefully draws the final pictures.

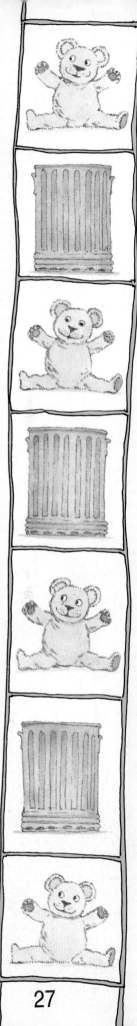

Surprising Riddles

Here are some riddles from all over the world. When you find the answers, you may be surprised!

A white house full of meat,
But no door to go in to eat.
What is it?
— from the United States

White as the clouds;
Yellow as the sun;
If I fall I break.
What am I?
— from Panama

All know how to open it;
Not one knows how to close it.
What is it?
— from Spain

Humpty Dumpty sat on a wall,
Humpty Dumpty had a great fall.
All the king's horses,
And all the king's men,
Couldn't put Humpty together again.
Who is Humpty Dumpty?
— from England

What is more useful when it is broken?
— from Jamaica

many riddles with the same answer?
Did you ever think there could be so
ANSWER: An egg.

29

SURPRISES

Surprises are round
    Or long and tallish.
Surprises are square
    Or flat and smallish.

Surprises are wrapped
    With paper and bow,
And hidden in closets
    Where secrets won't show.

Surprises are often
    Good things to eat;
A get-well toy or
    A birthday treat.

Surprises come
    In such interesting sizes —
I LIKE
    SURPRISES!

by Jean Conder Soule

FIX-IT

by David McPhail

One morning Emma got up early
to watch television.

But the TV didn't work.

Emma asked her mother to fix it.
"Hurry, Mom!" she cried.
Emma's mother tried to fix it.
But she couldn't.

Emma's father tried.

But he couldn't fix it, either.

So he called the fix-it man. "Please
hurry," he said. "It's an emergency!"

The fix-it man came right away.
He tried to fix the TV. Emma's mother
and father tried to fix Emma.

Her father blew up a balloon . . .

until it popped.

Her mother sang a song.
So did the cat.

Her father pretended to be a horse —
but Emma didn't feel like riding.

Finally her mother read her a book.

"Read it again," said Emma when her
mother had finished.

"And again."

"And again."

"Now *I'll* read to Millie," said Emma.
And she went to her room.

Then her father found out
what was wrong with the TV.
"I fixed it!" he called.
But Emma didn't come out
of her room.

She was too busy.

Books Can Be Surprising

Did Emma like the book her mother read to her? What makes you think so? Did it surprise you that Emma liked the book more than TV?

Make a list of books you like. Then surprise a friend. Give the list to your friend, and see if he or she wants to read any of the books.

David McPhail has always liked to draw. He started to draw before he was two years old! But, by the time he was ten, he didn't want to be an artist — he wanted to be a baseball player.

David McPhail never became a baseball player. Instead he has done many other things, such as work in a factory, play in a band, make arrows, and sell greeting cards. And best of all, he now writes and illustrates books for children.

Drinking Fountain

When I climb up
To get a drink,
It doesn't work
The way you'd think.

I turn it up,
The water goes
And hits me right
Upon the nose.

I turn it down
To make it small
And don't get any
Drink at all.

by Marchette Chute

43

This Tooth

I jiggled it
jaggled it
jerked it.

I pushed
and pulled
and poked it.

But—

As soon as I stopped,
And left it alone,
This tooth came out
on its very own!

by Lee Bennett Hopkins

44

How to Hide a Polar Bear

and Other Mammals

by *Ruth Heller*

If you take a careful look, you'll see how creatures in this book are CAMOUFLAGED and out of view — although they're right in front of you.

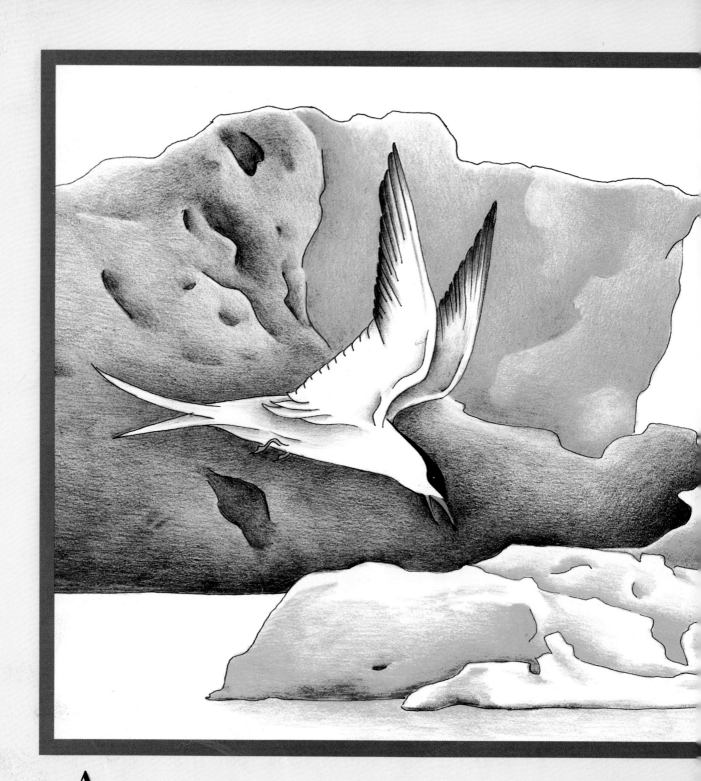

A POLAR BEAR will only go
where there is lots of ice and snow.

Its fur is always white, you know,
so it will hardly . . . even show.

The SNOWSHOE HARE is turning brown
because the snow is melting down,

and when there's only snow in patches
you will find that this hare . . . matches.

This dappled DEER will disappear

into the filtered sunlight . . . here.

A ZEBRA doesn't seem to be
a creature who hides easily,

but in the shade, behind a tree,
its silhouette is . . . hard to see.

53

The lazy LEOPARD likes to lie
upon a leafy limb,

where leaves and bark and sunshine
and his spots have . . . hidden him.

The color of the LION
and the color of his mane
and the color of the grass

that grows upon the plain
all . . . seem to be the same.

Because the SLOTH's so very slow,
green algae find the time to grow

and thrive upon its thick coarse hair.
Then you can hardly tell . . . it's there.

Do Like Kyla

by Angela Johnson

illustrated by James E. Ransome

In the morning my big sister Kyla
stands at the window, tapping at the
birds. I do like Kyla, only standing
on the bed.

Kyla pulls her sweater over her head
and stretches. I do like Kyla.

We sit in front of the big mirror in our room, and Kyla braids her hair with quick fingers. I try to do like Kyla in front of the mirror.

Kyla says, "Beautiful!"

I do like Kyla and say, "Beautiful!"

Oatmeal and apples for breakfast, and I
do like Kyla, pouring honey on everything.

Mama says, "Lots of sunshine today."
Kyla kisses the sunbeam on the dog's
head. I do like Kyla.

We're going to the store so Kyla helps
me put my coat on.

"Warm now," she says.

I do like Kyla and say, "Warm now."

Got me some purple snow boots like
Kyla, and we both crunch, crunch in the
snow all the way to the store.

Past the big store window, I see
myself. I do like Kyla and skip past the
window watching. . . .

In the good-smelling store Kyla asks for
cheese, a bag of apples, and a jar of jam.
   The man in the white apron says,
"Goodbye and be good."
   I do like Kyla and say, "OK, I will."

Kyla says, "Want to follow our
footsteps back home?"
I do, just like Kyla.
Step, step, step.

"Read me a book, Kyla."

Kyla reads to me under the kitchen table.

I do like her and say, "The end," after the last page.

It's almost nighttime at the window.
Kyla says, "Birds must be asleep."
I tap at the window . . . and Kyla does
just like me.

Surprisingly Special

What was the surprise at the end of the story? Do you think that Kyla was surprised to find herself copying what her sister did?

Think about why Kyla's sister wanted to be like her. Then think about someone whom you want to be like. Draw a picture and write about that person. Show a friend what you've done. Maybe they'll be surprised to see whom you want to copy!

Meet the Author

Angela Johnson comes from a family of storytellers. When they were children, she and her brothers listened to their grandfather and their father tell stories over and over again. They heard the stories so many times, she says, that they knew them by heart. Now, Mrs. Johnson has become a writer of stories. Her first picture book story was *Tell Me a Story, Mama.*

Meet the Illustrator

James E. Ransome went to art school and worked as an illustrator before he did the pictures for *Do Like Kyla.* He has been given awards for his artwork. Some other books he illustrated are *Aunt Flossie's Hats* and *How Many Stars in the Sky?*

The Cake That Mack Ate

by Rose Robart

What does it take to make a cake? Mack knows!

Daddy Has a Pair of Striped Shorts

by Mimi Otey

A girl is surprised to find out that other people see her father in a different way than she does.

What's Claude Doing?

by Dick Gackenbach

Claude is too busy to play with his friends. What could he be up to?

The Grumpalump

by Sarah Hayes

What is this grumpalump in the middle of a field? A bunch of curious animals are surprised when they find out what it is.

Scared Silly

Beware!!! Here are some tales that might make you feel scared silly! Get ready for some chills and thrills — and maybe some giggles, too. You never know what might be lurking on these pages!

82

Contents

Klippity Klop   84
written and illustrated by Ed Emberley

The Gunnywolf   119
written and illustrated by A. Delaney

Strange Bumps   134
from Owl at Home
written and illustrated by Arnold Lobel

KLIPPITY
KLOP

BY ED EMBERLEY

PRINCE KRISPIN
AND DUMPLING
WENT FOR A RIDE.

KLIPPITY·KLOP   KLIP·KLOP   KLIPPITY·KLOP

THEY CAME TO A BRIDGE
AND RODE OVER IT,

KLIPPITY KLOP KLIPPITY KLUMP KLUMPITY KLUMPIT

THEY CAME TO A STREAM
AND RODE ACROSS IT,

KLOP KLIPPITY KLOP · KERPLASH · KERPLOSH · KERPLASH · KERPLOSH · KERPLIS

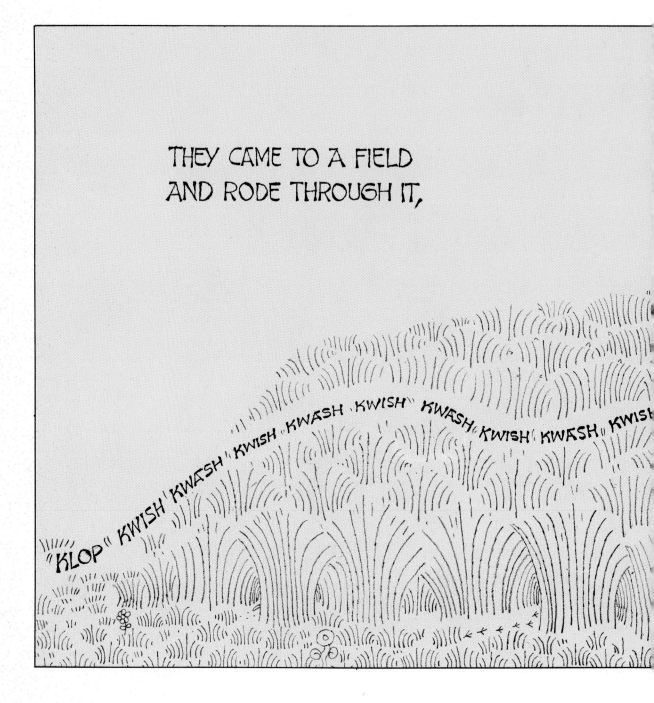

THEY CAME TO A FIELD
AND RODE THROUGH IT,

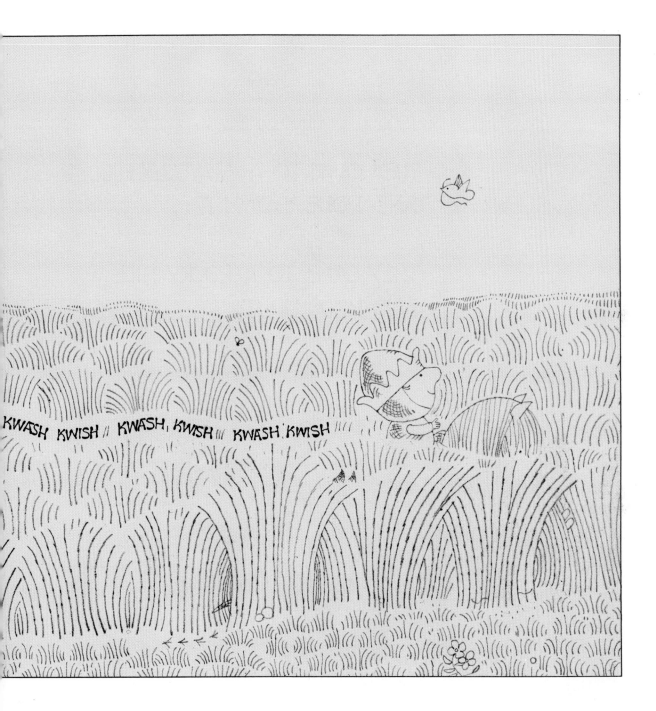

KWASH KWISH KWASH, KWISH KWASH KWISH

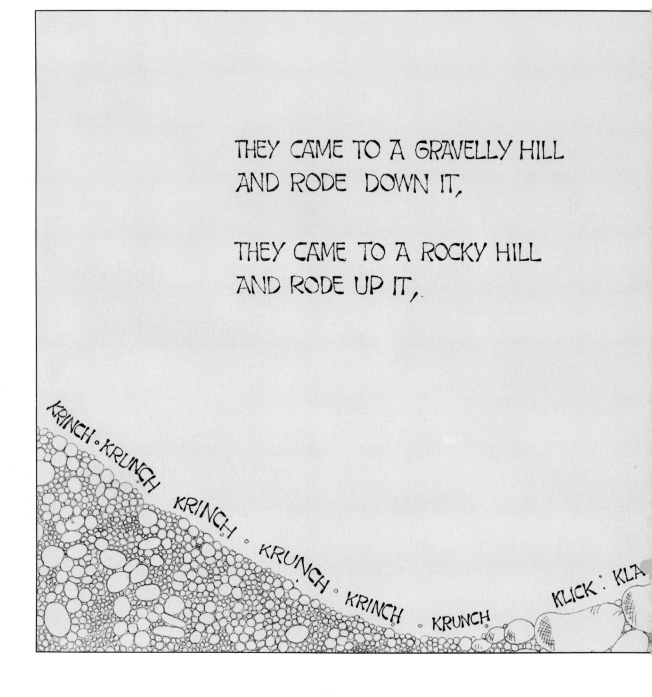

THEY CAME TO A GRAVELLY HILL
AND RODE DOWN IT,

THEY CAME TO A ROCKY HILL
AND RODE UP IT,

KRINCH · KRUNCH · KRINCH · KRUNCH · KRINCH · KRUNCH   KLICK : KLA

THEY CAME TO A CAVE
AND LOOKED IN...

KLACK . KLICK . KLACK . KLICK . KLACK . KLICK

A DRAGON
LOOKED OUT...

WELL!! THE DRAGON
DID NOT HAVE TO YELL TWICE.
DUMPLING TURNED AND RAN:

DOWN THE ROCKY HILL,
  UP THE GRAVELLY HILL,

KRINCHITY. KRUNCHITY. KRUNCHITY. KLACKITY

THROUGH THE FIELD,

KWISH KWISH KWISH KWISH KWISH KWISH KWISH KWISH KWISH KWISH
KWISH

ACROSS THE STREAM,

103

INTO THE CASTLE...
AND
CLOSED THE DOOR!

WHEW!
GOING ADVENTURING
IS A FINE THING...

If I Saw a Dragon . . .

What would you do if you saw a dragon? Would you act as Prince Krispin and Dumpling acted? Or would you do something else?

Tell how you would feel and what you would do if you met a dragon. Draw pictures, write a story, or do both.

Meet the Author and Illustrator

Ed Emberley wanted to draw pictures for children's books. But no one sent him stories to draw pictures for. Finally, he wrote his own book and drew pictures for it. People said that they liked it a lot.

Now Ed Emberley is a famous children's author. He and his wife, Barbara Emberley, made their barn into a workshop for writing and drawing. They work on books together in their workshop.

CHINESE DRAGONS

In some parts of the world, stories tell of fierce dragons who frighten people. In China, people think of dragons as strong but helpful creatures. Dragons are an important part of Chinese festivals and celebrations.

Chinese New Year

Many Chinese people live in the U.S.A. They like to enjoy their New Year in the old Chinese way. They perform a Dragon Dance as they carry a beautiful paper dragon through the streets.

Wherever the dragon goes, it brings peace and good luck. The people set off firecrackers. These are meant to scare away evil spirits. The festival goes on into the night.

— from Festivals Around the World

龍 Written words in Chinese are called characters. The Chinese word dragon looks like this. Can you see a dragon's head and tail in the character?

Catching the Dragon's Tail

Chinese children have fun with this dragon game. Maybe you and your friends would like to try it.

Number of players: Ten or more.

Formation: All players stand in a line, their hands on one another's shoulders. The first person in line is the head of the dragon, and the last is the tail.

Action: The head tries to catch the tail by maneuvering the line around so that he or she can tag the end player. The line must not break. All the other players do their best to keep the head from catching the dragon's tail. When the head catches the tail, the end player becomes the new head and the player who was in front of him or her becomes the tail.

— from Games of Many Nations

Dragon Boats

This Chinese nursery rhyme tells about boats decorated to look like dragons. These boats are raced during the Dragon Festival held in early summer.

The dragon boats! There they go!
Beat the drums! Row and row!
The swiftest dragon in the race
Will be the dragon in first place!

— from Dragon Kites and Dragonflies: A Collection of Chinese Nursery Rhymes

A LONG-HAIRED GRIGGLE

A long-haired Griggle from the land of Grunch
Always giggled when he ate his lunch.
He'd wiggle and giggle, and munch and crunch
While nibbling the pebbles that he liked for lunch.

Alice Gilbert

THE GUNNYWOLF

RETOLD AND ILLUSTRATED BY A. DELANEY

Once upon a time, a Little Girl and
her father lived next to a deep, dark woods.

The Little Girl never went into the woods.

Nobody did. The Gunnywolf lived there.

But one day, the Little Girl saw a flower
blooming just inside the woods.

The Little Girl forgot all about the Gunnywolf.
She stepped between the trees
and picked the flower.

And she sang,
"A B C D E F G
H I J K L M N O P
Q R S T U V
W X Y Z."

When the Little Girl looked up, she saw more
flowers. Again she forgot about the Gunnywolf.

The Little Girl skipped deeper into the
woods and picked the flowers.

And she sang,
"A B C D E F G H I J K L M N O P Q R S T U V —"

When the Little Girl looked up,
she saw even more flowers.

Again she forgot about the Gunnywolf.

The Little Girl ran deep into the woods and
picked the flowers. And she sang,
"A B C D E F G H I J K L
M N O P —"

The Little Girl was far from home.
Holding her flowers, she turned to go, and —

THERE WAS THE GUNNYWOLF!

"Little Girl!" said the Gunnywolf.
"Sing that good, sweet song to me."

"abcdefghijklmnopqrstuvwxyz,"
sang the Little Girl in a tiny voice.

"M
  M
    N
      A
        B,"
sang the Gunnywolf,
and he fell sound asleep.

The Little Girl ran away as fast as she could.
Pit-a-pat, pit-a-pat, pit-a-pat, pit-a-pat!

The Gunnywolf woke up!

Un-ka-cha! Un-ka-cha! Un-ka-cha! Un-ka-cha!
He ran, and soon he caught up with the Little Girl.

"Little Girl!" said the Gunnywolf.
"Sing that good, sweet song again."

"A B C D E F G H I J K L M N O P Q R
S T U V W X Y Z," sang the Little Girl.

"Q
 R
  L
   S
    P," sang the Gunnywolf,
and he fell sound asleep.

Pit-a-pat, pit-a-pat, pit-a-pat, pit-a-pat!

The Little Girl ran back through the woods
as fast as she could.

The Gunnywolf woke up!
Un-ka-cha!   Un-ka-cha!
Un-ka-cha!
Un-ka-cha!

He ran, and again he caught up with the Little Girl.

"Little Girl!" said the Gunnywolf.
"Sing that good, sweet song again."

"A B C D E F G H I J K L M N O P
Q R S T U V W X Y Z," sang the Little Girl.

"X
 Y
  Z
   Z
    z,"

sang the Gunnywolf, and he fell sound asleep.

Pit-a-pat, pit-a-pat, pit-a-pat, pit-a-pat!
The Little Girl ran out of the woods.

"Whew!" said the Little Girl.

But the next day and every day after that,
when the Little Girl went outside,
she gathered flowers and more flowers
and even more flowers.

And she sang,
"A B C D E F G
H I J K L M N O P
Q R S T U V
W X Y Z."

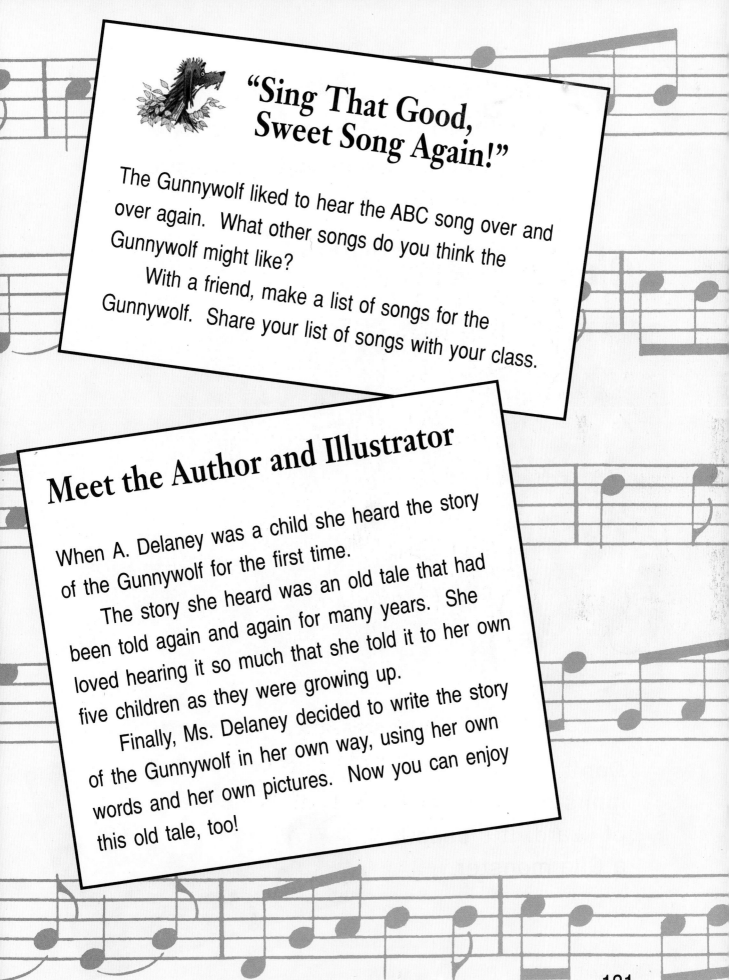

"Sing That Good, Sweet Song Again!"

The Gunnywolf liked to hear the ABC song over and over again. What other songs do you think the Gunnywolf might like?

With a friend, make a list of songs for the Gunnywolf. Share your list of songs with your class.

Meet the Author and Illustrator

When A. Delaney was a child she heard the story of the Gunnywolf for the first time.

The story she heard was an old tale that had been told again and again for many years. She loved hearing it so much that she told it to her own five children as they were growing up.

Finally, Ms. Delaney decided to write the story of the Gunnywolf in her own way, using her own words and her own pictures. Now you can enjoy this old tale, too!

Monsters and Dragons

Oh no! It's a monster!

Don't worry — this monster is only a kind of lizard. It's called a Gila monster.

Look out! Here comes a dragon!

This dragon doesn't breathe fire. It's a Komodo dragon. A Komodo dragon is a lizard, too.

Why do you think people call these lizards *Gila monsters* and *Komodo dragons*?

A story from
OWL AT HOME
by Arnold Lobel

Strange Bumps

Owl was in bed.

"It is time

to blow out the candle

and go to sleep,"

he said with a yawn.

Then Owl saw two bumps

under the blanket

at the bottom of his bed.

"What can those strange bumps

be?" asked Owl.

Owl lifted up the blanket.

He looked down into the bed.

All he could see was darkness.

Owl tried to sleep,

but he could not.

"What if those

two strange bumps

grow bigger and bigger

while I am asleep?"

said Owl.

"That would not be pleasant."

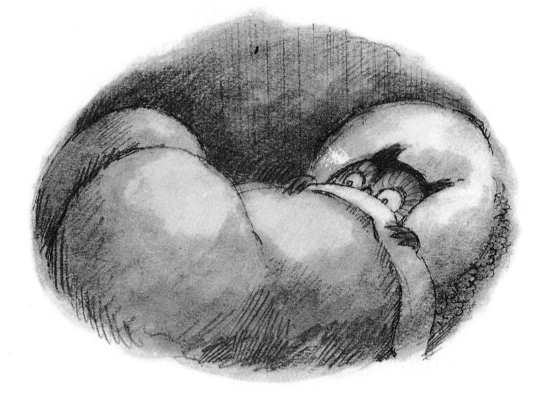

Owl moved his right foot

up and down.

The bump on the right

moved up and down.

"One of those bumps

is moving!" said Owl.

Owl moved his left foot

up and down.

The bump

on the left

moved up and down.

"The other bump is moving!"

cried Owl.

Owl pulled

all of the covers

off his bed.

The bumps were gone.

All Owl could see

at the bottom of the bed

were his own two feet.

"But now I am cold,"

said Owl.

"I will cover myself

with the blankets again."

As soon as he did,

he saw the same two bumps.

"Those bumps are back!"

shouted Owl.

"Bumps, bumps, bumps!

I will never sleep tonight!"

Owl jumped

up and down

on top of his bed.

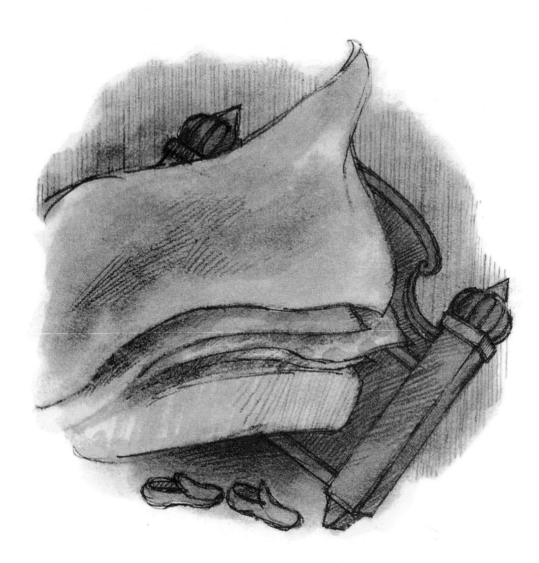

"Where are you?

What are you?" he cried.

With a crash and a bang

the bed came falling down.

Owl ran

down the stairs.

He sat in his chair

near the fire.

"I will let those two strange bumps

sit on my bed

all by themselves,"

said Owl.

"Let them grow

as big as they wish.

I will sleep right here

where I am safe."

And that is what he did.

Hello, It's Owl

Talking with a friend about scary things sometimes makes them seem less scary.

What would you say if Owl called to tell you about the strange bumps? With a friend, act out a phone call with Owl.

Meet the Author and Illustrator

Lobel

Arnold Lobel liked to draw so much that he drew pictures for almost 100 children's books. He liked to write funny stories about animals.

Frog, Toad, and Owl are some of the animals that Arnold Lobel wrote about. He once said that the ideas for his stories came from his own life — sometimes he felt like Frog, sometimes like Toad, and sometimes like Owl.

The Monster Stomp

by John Perry

If you want to be a monster, now's your chance
'Cause everybody's doing the monster dance.

**You just stamp
your feet,**

**Wave your
arms around,**

**Stretch 'em up,
stretch 'em up,**

**Then put them
on the ground,**

'Cause you're doing the monster stomp,
That's right, you're doing the monster stomp.
Ooh–Ah–Ooh–Ah–Ooh–Ah–Ooh–Ah!
Ooh–Ah–Ooh–Ah–Ooh–Ah–Ooh–Ah!

More Scared Silly Stories

Monster Tracks? *by A. Delaney*
Who or what could make such big tracks in the snow? Harry bravely follows the tracks into the woods to find out.

I Am Scared *by Ivar Da Coll*
Eusebio the tiger is scared of monsters. Can Ananías the duck help him?

We're Going on a Bear Hunt

by Michael Rosen

A happy family sets off on a great adventure. What do you think happens when they find what they're looking for?

Morton and Sidney *by Chris Demarest*

Why is Sidney, a friendly monster, out in the daytime? He belongs in Morton's closet until nighttime.

149

CATS

There are many different kinds of cats.
Some are wild, and some are tame. Some live
as pets with people. Some live in jungles or on
mountains. And some may live only in our
imagination.

Here are some stories, poems, and jokes
about all kinds of cats.

CONTENTS

No One Should Have Six Cats! 154
by Susan Mathias Smith
illustrated by Steff Geissbuhler

Tiger Runs 176
by Derek Hall
illustrated by John Butler

Chitina and Her Cat 192
by Montserrat del Amo
illustrated by Denise
and Fernando

No One

Should Have

Six Cats!

by Susan Mathias Smith
illustrated by Steff Geissbuhler

We have six cats at my house. But soon that will change.

This morning my mom told me, "No one should have six cats, David."

I can tell that Mom thinks I should give one cat away. But which one? I love them all.

Herkie is cat number one. I found him in an alley one day. He had a hurt paw. He looked so sad and lonely.

Nobody knew where Herkie lived.

And nobody wanted him.

What could I do?

I had no choice.

I let him live with us.

Now Herkie's paw is all better. He can run and play and climb trees.

He and I are good friends.

I just can't give my Herkie away.

160

Zip is cat number two. She was sleeping
near the bank on King Street when I found her.

Nobody knew where Zip lived.

And nobody wanted her.

What could I do?

I had no choice.

I let her live with us.

Zip doesn't do much except sleep and eat.
But she's a happy cat. And whenever she's
awake, she purrs.

I just can't give my Zip away.

Shadow is cat number three. I didn't find Shadow. He found me. One cold, snowy day he moved into our garage. There were some old newspapers stacked in a corner. Shadow used them as his bed.

Nobody knew where Shadow came from.

And nobody wanted him.

What else could I do?

I had no choice.

I let him live with us.

Shadow is afraid of most people. But he's not afraid of me. He lets me hold him close and pet him.

I just can't give my Shadow away.

Tinker is cat number four. She used to belong to my cousins. But last summer they had to move away. They couldn't take Tinker with them.

Nobody knew where Tinker would live.
And nobody wanted her.
What else could I do?
I had no choice.
I let her live with us.
Tinker sleeps under my bed. Every morning she licks my face and wakes me up.
I just can't give my Tinker away.

166

Boots is cat number five. I found him near the playground. He was just a kitten then. He was so little and afraid.

Nobody knew where Boots lived.

And nobody wanted him.

What could I do?

I had no choice.

I let him live with us.

Boots was too little to drink milk from a dish. So I fed him from a baby bottle. I saw him grow and grow. Now he is a big and beautiful cat.

I just can't give my Boots away.

Hairy is cat number six. Hairy once lived
with Belinda, my friend at school. But
Belinda's sister has a problem with cats. They
make her sneeze.

So Belinda couldn't keep Hairy.

And nobody wanted him.

What could I do?

I had no choice.

I let him live with us.

At first, Hairy did not like my other cats.
He would tease them and get them angry. But
now Hairy and the others play and have fun
together.

I just can't give my Hairy away.

What will I do?

Here comes my mom home from work now. She will say, "No one should have six cats, David. Not even us."

But I don't know which cat I want to give away.

"Mom, what do you have?" I ask. "Is that a little kitten?"

"Yes," answers Mom. "I found her outside of the office. Nobody knew where she came from. And nobody wanted her. What could I do? I had no choice. I've decided to let her live with us."

"But, Mom, you told me that no one should have six cats. Not even us," I say.

"That's right," Mom tells me. "No one should have six cats. Instead of having six cats, we should have seven!"

How About Seven Cats?

Now David and his mother have seven cats. That's a lot of cats!

Do you think you would like to have seven cats? What would be nice about it? What would be some of the problems?

Get together with a few friends to talk about having seven cats. You can make two lists — one list for the nice things and one list for the problems.

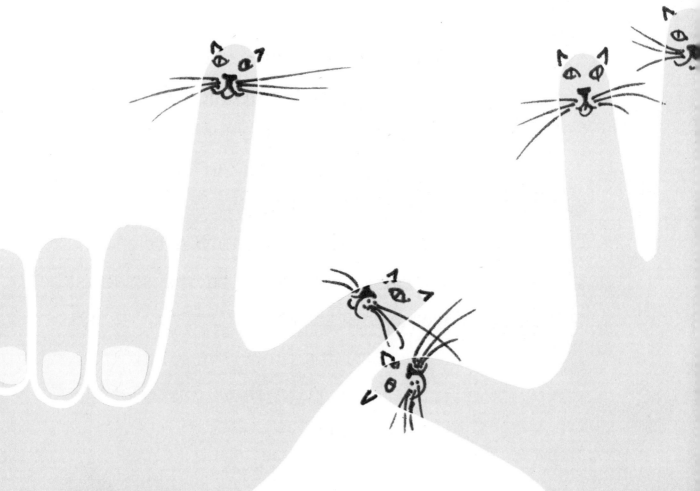

Meet the Author

Susan Mathias Smith loves animals. Maybe that is why most of the children's books she writes are about animals. She says she wants her stories to help children love and care for pets.

She says, "Sometimes when I cannot think of ideas or when I am discouraged, I go to the library and read children's books. I read until I laugh or smile. . . . Then I drive home and I think and I write."

Meet the Illustrator

Steff Geissbuhler has had pet cats ever since he was a little boy. He now has a cat named Sly.

Mr. Geissbuhler likes to draw cats and other animals. He works for a graphic design company where he creates posters and signs for museums, schools, and businesses.

Favorite Poems, Favorite Cats

At Night
by Aileen Fisher

When night is dark
my cat is wise
to light the lanterns
in his eyes.

Cats Sleep Anywhere
by Eleanor Farjeon

Cats sleep
Anywhere,
Any table,
Any chair,
Top of piano,
Window-ledge,
In the middle,
On the edge,
Open drawer,
Empty shoe,

Anybody's
Lap will do,
Fitted in a
Cardboard box,
In the cupboard
With your frocks —
Anywhere!
They don't care!
Cats sleep
Anywhere.

The House Cat
by Annette Wynne

The house cat sits

And smiles and sings.

He knows a lot

Of secret things.

Cat Kisses
by Bobbi Katz

Sandpaper kisses
on a cheek or a chin —
that is the way
for a day to begin!

Sandpaper kisses —
a cuddle, a purr.
I have an alarm clock
that's covered with fur.

Tiger Runs

by Derek Hall

illustrated by John Butler

Tiger is feeling so bored. Her mother
has gone hunting for food. Hunting is very
dangerous, so Tiger must stay in a safe place.

Tiger wants to play. What's that?
Something is moving in the grass. She trots
over to see. It's a beautiful butterfly.

Tiger tries to touch the butterfly, but it
darts away. She scampers after it. Again and
again she tries to catch it with her paw.

Tiger is lost! She has chased the butterfly
for such a long way. And now it is raining.
She sits down and cries like a kitten.

Suddenly, there's a noise! Tiger looks up, frightened. A huge elephant is lumbering towards her. It's the biggest animal she has ever seen.

Tiger turns and runs, faster than she has
ever run before. She is running like the wind,
and crying for her mother.

Tiger hears her mother's roar, and runs to meet her. Tiger's mother is very cross. But Tiger is so pleased to see her again.

Tiger's mother soon forgives her. They lie down, and Tiger climbs on to her. She purrs happily, feeling safe once more.

JUNGLE PLAY

What animals are in *Tiger Runs*?

How do these animals move?

What sounds do they make?

Get together with some friends to act out the story in *Tiger Runs*. Try to do it without using words.

Meet the Author

Derek Hall has written many books for children. His books tell about young animals and how they grow up. Here are some of the other books he has written: *Elephant Bathes, Gorilla Builds, Polar Bear Leaps, Otter Swims,* and *Panda Climbs.*

Meet the Illustrator

John Butler has always liked watching and drawing animals. When he was a boy, he would often take care of sick birds and other animals.

When he wasn't spending time with animals, he was reading books about them. He says, "I can remember studying all the illustrations and imagining the lives the animals lived."

LIONS

Lion

by N. M. Bodecker

The lion,
when he r o a r s
at night,
gives many people
quite
a fright!

The lion,
when he r o a r s
by day,
scares people near
him
far
away.

And when
he sleeps,
his lion s n o r e
is quite as scary as
his
r o a r.

TIGERS

The Tiger
by *Ernesto Galarza*
translated from Spanish

The tiger, no!

Never touch, no!

Not his tail, no!

Not his nose, no!

Don't be curious, no!

He'll be furious —

Yes!

All Kinds

Cats have whiskers.

tiger

pet

Cats have paws.

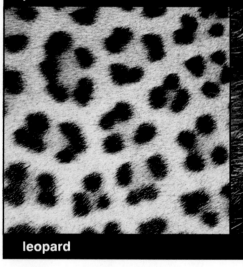

pet

lion

Cats have soft fur.

leopard

pet

lioness

pet

Cats run
and leap.

pet

black panther

Cats can
climb trees.

lion

pet

And all cats,
everywhere,
like to sleep
in the sun!

192

CHITINA
AND HER CAT

by Montserrat del Amo
illustrated by Denise and Fernando

◆ ◆ ◆

Chitina had a cat named Almost. He was almost as black as coal. He was almost as striped as a tiger.

Chitina and Almost were good friends. Every day they played together. Every night Almost slept in a basket at the foot of Chitina's bed. When Chitina woke up in the night, she could hear Almost purring. It helped her go back to sleep.

One night Chitina woke up and called very softly, "Almost!"

On most nights, Almost would come running as soon as Chitina called. But that night he did not come.

Chitina called again, this time a little louder: "Almost!" There was still no answer.

Chitina turned on the light. The cat basket was empty. Chitina looked all over the bedroom for Almost. She looked in her toy box. She looked under her dresser. Almost was nowhere to be found.

"He must be in the garden," she thought.

Chitina tiptoed across the hallway and down the stairs. Then she stepped out into the garden. It was dark. Chitina was scared. She closed her eyes and called again: "Almost!"

The sound of her own voice scared her even more. She covered her ears with her hands. And she called again: "Almost! Where are you?"

Chitina felt a tug. It felt as if someone was holding onto her nightshirt. She tried to pull away, but she could not get free.

Chitina stood very still. Her eyes were shut and her hands were over her ears.

"I don't want to stay here like this," she thought to herself. Slowly she felt where her nightshirt was held. But there was no one there. Her nightshirt was caught on a branch.

Chitina began to pull her nightshirt free. She could tell the branch was part of a rosebush. She could smell the sweet smell of the roses on her hands. Suddenly all the things in the night began to speak to her.

"What are you doing out here in the darkness, little girl?" asked the stars.

"You should be in your bed sleeping!" said the moon.

"Why are your eyes closed?" asked a firefly on the rosebush.

Chitina told the truth. "It's very dark out here and I'm scared."

The stars laughed. "But you cannot see our starlight if your eyes are closed!"

Chitina opened her eyes. It was true. The night was filled with lights. The moon beamed, the stars twinkled, the fireflies winked. Even the flowers seemed to shine.

"What are you doing out here?" the stars asked again.

"I'm looking for Almost, my cat. He has disappeared," Chitina said.

"We will help you find him," the night things told her.

Then the stars became even brighter. The moon grew bigger and rounder. The wind went everywhere, calling "Almost!" The flowers sent out their sweet smell. The fireflies turned on their tiny lights, showing the way home.

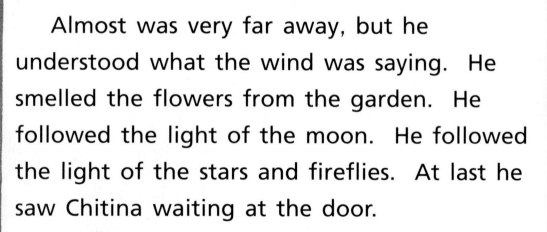

Almost was very far away, but he understood what the wind was saying. He smelled the flowers from the garden. He followed the light of the moon. He followed the light of the stars and fireflies. At last he saw Chitina waiting at the door.

Chitina took the cat in her arms. "Thank you, night," she said.

And this is what happened to a cat named Almost, who was almost as black as coal and almost as striped as a tiger. And to Chitina, who got really scared . . . well, almost!

What Would Almost Say?

Chitina imagined that she heard the moon, the stars, and the fireflies speak to her. What if she imagined that her cat could speak to her, too? What might Almost tell Chitina about what he saw the night he was lost?

Work with a partner to act out what Chitina and Almost might have said to each other when Almost got back home. Draw a picture to illustrate Almost's adventure, and share it with others in your class.

Meet the Author

Montserrat del Amo has written award-winning books, poetry, and plays for young people. Some of her stories, like *Chitina and Her Cat,* are about make-believe characters and events. Other stories are biographies, which tell about the lives of real people.

Montserrat del Amo writes in Spanish and lives in Spain.

Meet the Illustrators

Denise Fraifeld and Fernando Azevedo are from Brazil. Now they live and work in the United States. Several of the nearly thirty children's books they have illustrated have received awards. Even though they didn't plan to be artists, Denise and Fernando both loved to draw all the time when they were children.

CAT'S OUT OF THE BAG

by Sharon Friedman and Irene Shere

What's kitty's favorite subject in school?

Where did the cat get his new toaster?

What kind of music do cats like?

What did the cat say when he fell on his face?

What kind of cat lives under water?

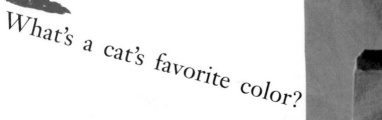

What's a cat's favorite color?

 A catfish.

 Mew-sic.

 Me-OW!

 From a cat-alog.

Purr-ple.

Cat-chy tunes.

209

Purr-fect Books

Charles Tiger
by Siobhan Dodds

Poor Charles Tiger
has lost his roar.
Where do you think
he will find it?

Young Lions
by Toshi Yoshida

Take a walk in Africa
with three lion cubs
on their first hunt.

The Rescue of Aunt Pansy

by Lisa Campbell Ernst

Joanne the mouse bravely rescues her Aunt Pansy from the cat. But wait — maybe it's not her aunt after all!

I Had a Cat

by Mona Rabun Reeves

This girl has a cat, a dog, and even a moose! But which does she love best?

Who Can Fix It?

Some people buy things. Some people sell things. Some people build things. Some people **fix** things that are broken.

In this lesson you will learn about people who fix things and about the **tools** that they use.

Thinking It Over

People have many different kinds of jobs. What kinds of jobs do you know about?

Key Words

fix
tools

Walter Grant lives on Red Bird Road. His car won't start. He'll be late for work. He calls Robert Yee to help him.

Robert Yee is a car mechanic. He brings his tools to Walter Grant's house. He tests the car battery. He tells Walter Grant that his car needs a new battery.

Robert Yee uses a screwdriver to take the screws off the battery. He uses pliers to twist the nuts off the bolts. Then he puts in a new battery. Now Walter Grant can go to work.

Stop and Think

1. What did Robert Yee fix?
2. What tools did he use?

Rita and Joe Ortega live next door to Mr. Grant. Tonight it's Rita's turn to wash the dishes. It's Joe's turn to dry them.

Rita turns on the water in the sink. Then she tries to turn off the water. The water keeps running out of the faucet! To make things worse, the sink is stopped up.

"Quick!" says Joe. "Call the plumber!"

Donald Ives is a plumber. He can fix the sink with his tools. He brings his tools to the Ortega house.

Donald Ives uses a wrench to tighten the pipes. The water stops running.

He also uses a long wire called a snake to clean out the pipes. The water will drain out of the sink quickly now.

Stop and Think

1. What needed to be fixed?
2. How did Donald Ives fix it?
3. What tools did he use?
4. What other things do you think a plumber could fix?

Cindy Levine and David Grant are neighbors on Red Bird Road. They are playing baseball in front of Cindy's house. It is Cindy's turn at bat.

David throws the ball to Cindy. Cindy hits it hard. The ball is heading for her house.

Oh, no! It crashes through her bedroom window!

Stop and Think

1. What needs to be fixed?
2. How do you think it can be fixed?

Jill Peters is a glazier. She can fix the window with her tools. She brings them to Cindy's house.

Jill Peters uses a small hammer to knock out the broken glass. Then she puts in a new pane of glass. She uses a putty knife to spread the putty. The putty holds the glass in place. The window is fixed.

"That was a nice home run," Jill Peters tells Cindy. "But next time, don't hit it so close to home!"

Review

1. What are some things people fix in their jobs?

2. What are some tools you learned about?

3. Has someone ever fixed something for you or your family? What tools did that person use?

Glossary

A

angry   Jill is **angry** with Fred. She is mad because he lost her book.

B

balloon   A **balloon** is a kind of toy. You can fill a **balloon** with air to make it bigger: Lee will blow up the big red **balloon**.

blanket   A **blanket** is a big piece of cloth. It covers you and keeps you warm: Susan got cold, so she put a **blanket** on her bed.

bump

1. If something falls with a **bump,** it makes a noise: I heard the book fall. It fell with a **bump**. **2.** A **bump** is a small hill: There were two big **bumps** under my blanket. They were my two cats!

C

castle

A **castle** is a big building: The king and queen lived in a **castle**.

cross

1. When you are **cross**, you are angry: Andy is **cross** because the dog ran off with his ball.
2. When you **cross** the room, you go from one side to the other: Maria and James are careful when they **cross** the street.

dragon

A **dragon** is a make-believe animal that is big and scary: Holly read about a **dragon** in her book.

dump   A **dump** is a place where you can throw out broken or unwanted things: Joan went to the **dump** to throw out her trash.

emergency The house was on fire, so the family got out right away. They called the firefighters and said, "This is an **emergency**! Come right away!"

empty   When something is **empty**, it has nothing in it: My glass is **empty** and yours is full.

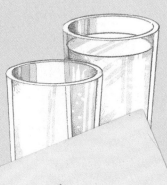

except   Jan was the only one at home. Everyone
               was gone **except** Jan.

finished   Teresa read the last page of the book.
               After she **finished** reading it, she took a
               walk.

frightened When you are scared, you are
               frightened: Carl gets
               frightened in the dark, so he
               turns on the light.

garage   A **garage** is a building where a car is parked: Mom drove the car into the **garage** for the night.

grass   **Grass** is a green plant. Sometimes **grass** can be brown. **Grass** grows in yards and parks: People mow **grass** when it grows tall.

hear   You **hear** with your ears: Can you **hear** the birds singing in the trees?

honey   **Honey** comes from bees and it tastes sweet: I pour **honey** on my toast. Toast and **honey** are good to eat.

instead   Roy wanted an apple, but we didn't have any. So he had an orange **instead.**

jar   A **jar** is made of glass. It can be used to hold many things: Jam and pickles come in **jars.**

kitten   A **kitten** is a baby cat: Luis has one big white cat and one little black **kitten.**

leopard   A **leopard** is a kind of wild cat with spotted fur: A **leopard** has spots, but a tiger has stripes.

mirror   A **mirror** is a shiny glass you can see yourself in: Sara looked in a **mirror** as she brushed her hair.

neat **1.** Greg cleaned his room and put away all of his toys. Now his room is as **neat** as a pin. **2.** The movie was really **neat**. It was really special.

noise A **noise** is a sound: The loud **noise** she heard was a ringing bell.

O

oatmeal **Oatmeal** is a kind of cooked cereal: David likes to eat **oatmeal** for breakfast.

P

paw   People have feet and hands. Cats and dogs have **paws**: The cat is all black with one white **paw**.

pleasant   If something is **pleasant**, it is nice: Mom and I took a **pleasant** walk on the beach.

purr   A **purr** is a sound that cats make: My cat **purrs** loudly whenever I pet her.

Q

quick   **Quick** is fast: Alice ran very fast. She was as **quick** as a rabbit.

right

1. I was sick yesterday, but now I feel all **right**. **2.** If we don't leave now, we will be late. We have to leave **right** away.

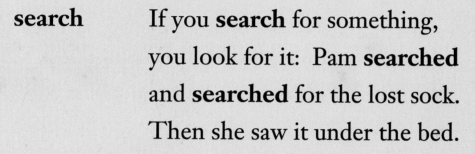

search

If you **search** for something, you look for it: Pam **searched** and **searched** for the lost sock. Then she saw it under the bed.

sound

1. When you are **sound** asleep, it is hard to wake you up: Hugo was very tired and quickly fell **sound** asleep. **2.** A **sound** is also what you hear: Do you hear that ringing **sound**?

strange   If something is **strange**, it is unusual or different: The animal in the picture is green and yellow. "What can that **strange** animal be?" asked Andy.

sweet   A nice or pleasing person, animal, or thing can be called **sweet:** Whenever I hear that **sweet** song, it makes me feel happy and peaceful.

T

television   You can see pictures and hear sounds on a **television:** Do you watch shows on **television** after school?

touch   Carla may **touch** the ice with her fingers. The ice will make her fingers feel cold.

under   My cat was hiding **under** the rug. He made a big bump in it.

voice   When you talk, you use your **voice**: I could hear Lisa's loud **voice** all the way upstairs.

whew   The king raced away from the dragon and into the castle. "**Whew**!" he exclaimed. "I got inside just in time!"

woods   **Woods** are places where lots of trees grow close together: Shan saw many small animals and birds on her hike through the **woods**.

yell   When you **yell,** you talk very loudly: Tommy **yelled** across the playground to Kim.

zebra   A **zebra** is a wild animal. A **zebra** looks like a white horse with black stripes.

Acknowledgments

For each of the selections listed below, grateful acknowledgment is made for permission to excerpt and/or reprint original or copyrighted material, as follows:

Major Selections

Chitina and Her Cat (*Chitina y su Gato*), by Montserrat del Amo. Copyright © Editorial Juventud, Barcelona, Spain, 1976. Translated and reprinted by permission of Editorial Juventud, S.A.

Do Like Kyla, by Angela Johnson, paintings by James E. Ransome. Text copyright © 1990 by Angela Johnson. Paintings copyright © 1990 by James E. Ransome. All rights reserved. Reprinted by permission of Orchard Books, New York.

Fix-It, by David McPhail. Copyright © 1984 by David McPhail. Reprinted by permission of Dutton Children's Books (a division of Penguin Books USA, Inc.).

The Gunnywolf, by A. Delaney. Copyright © 1988 by A. Delaney. Reprinted by permission of Harper and Row, Publishers, Inc.

How to Hide a Polar Bear and Other Mammals, by Ruth Heller. Copyright © 1985 by Ruth Heller. Reprinted by permission of Grosset & Dunlap.

Klippity Klop, by Ed Emberley. Copyright © 1974 by Edward R. Emberley. Reprinted by permission of Little, Brown and Company.

No One Should Have Six Cats! by Susan Mathias Smith. Copyright © 1982 by Susan Mathias Smith. Reprinted by permission of Modern Curriculum Press, Inc.

"Strange Bumps," from *Owl at Home* by Arnold Lobel. Copyright © 1975 by Arnold Lobel. Reprinted by permission of Harper and Row, Publishers, Inc.

This Is the Bear, by Sarah Hayes, illustrated by Helen Craig. (Lippincott) Text copyright © 1986 by Sarah Hayes. Illustrations copyright © 1986 by Helen Craig. Reprinted by permission of Harper and Row, Publishers, Inc.

Tiger Runs, by Derek Hall, illustrated by John Butler. Text copyright © 1984 by Derek Hall. Illustrations copyright © 1984 by John Butler. Reprinted by permission of Walker Books Limited.

Poetry

"At Night," from *Out in the Dark and Daylight* by Aileen Fisher. Text copyright © 1980 by Aileen Fisher. Reprinted by permission of Harper and Row, Publishers, Inc.

"Cat Kisses," by Bobbi Katz. Copyright © 1974 by Bobbi Katz. Used with permission of the author.

"Catching the Dragon's Tail," text adapted from *Games of Many Nations* by E.O. Harbin. Copyright © 1982 by Elizabeth Harbin Standish and Thomas Harbin. Reprinted by permission of Abingdon Press.

"Cats Sleep Anywhere," from *Eleanor Farjeon's Poems for Children* by Eleanor Farjeon. Originally appeared in *Sing for Your Supper* by Eleanor Farjeon. Copyright © 1938 by Eleanor Farjeon, renewed 1966 by Gervase Farjeon. Reprinted by permission of Harper and Row, Publishers, Inc.

"Chinese New Year in San Francisco, USA," from *Festivals Around the World* by Philip Steele. Copyright © 1986 by Dillon Press, Inc. Reprinted by permission of Heinemann Children's Reference.

"Drinking Fountain," from *Around and About* by Marchette Chute. Copyright © 1957 by E. P. Dutton, renewed 1985 by Marchette Chute. Reprinted by permission of Mary Chute Smith.

"The House Cat," from *For Days and Days* by Annette Wynne. (Lippincott) Copyright © 1919 by J. B. Lippincott Company, renewed 1947 by Annette Wynne. Reprinted by permission of Harper and Row, Publishers, Inc.

"The dragon boats! . . ." from *Dragon Kites and Dragonflies: A Collection of Chinese Nursery Rhymes* adapted and illustrated by Demi. Copyright © 1986 by Demi. Reprinted by permission of Harcourt Brace Jovanovich, Inc. and Curtis Brown Ltd.

"Lion," from *Snowman Sniffles* by N. M. Bodecker. Copyright © 1982 by N. M. Bodecker (a Margaret K. McElderry Book). Reprinted by permission.

"A Long-haired Griggle," from *Poems for Sharon's Lunch Box* by Alice Gilbert. Copyright © 1972 by Alice Gilbert. Reprinted by permission of the author.

Riddles from Jamaica, Panama, Spain, and the United States, in *Laughing Together: Giggles and Grins from Around the Globe* by Barbara K. Walker. Copyright © 1992. Reprinted by permission of Free Spirit Publishing, Inc. All rights reserved.

"Surprises," by Jean Conder Soule. Copyright © 1983 by Jean Conder Soule. Reprinted by permission of the author.

"The Tiger" ("El Tigre"), by Ernesto Galarza. Copyright © 1971 by Ernesto Galarza. Reprinted by permission of Mae Galarza.

"This Tooth," from *More Surprises* by Lee Bennett Hopkins. Copyright © 1970 by Lee Bennett Hopkins. Reprinted by permission of Curtis Brown, Ltd.

Others

"Cat's Out of the Bag!" by Sharon Friedman and Irene Shere. Copyright © 1986 by Lerner Publications. Reprinted by permission of the publisher.

The first verse of "The Monster Stomp," by John Perry, from *Game-songs With Prof. Dogg's Troup*. Copyright © 1983. Reprinted by permission of A & C Black (Publishers) Ltd. in association with Inter-Action Imprint.

Credits

Program Design   Carbone Smolan Associates

Cover Design   Carbone Smolan Associates

Design   10–77 Studio Izbickas;   80–149 Carbone Smolan Associates;   150–191, 208–211 Chermayeff & Geismar;   192–207 Carbone Smolan Associates;   212–217 DECODE

Introduction   (left to right) 1st row: Steff Geissbuhler; Frank Siteman; Roni Shepherd;   2nd row. *Animals Animals* © Michael P. Gadomski; Alyssa Adams; Ray Cruz;   3rd row: Steff Geissbuhler; Superstock; John Lei;   4th row: Frank Siteman; Doreen Gay-Kassel; Bruce Coleman Inc./Rod Williams

Table of Contents   4 Roni Shepherd;   6 Doreen Gay-Kassel;   8 Steff Geissbuhler

Illustration   11 David McPhail;   12–13 Roni Shepherd;   14–25 Helen Craig;   26 Valerie McKeown;   27 Helen Craig;   28–29 Ray Cruz;   30 Patrick Chapin;   31–40, 42 David McPhail;   44 Studio Izbickas;   45–59 Ruth Heller;   60–75 James E. Ransome;   80–83 Alyssa Adams;   84–112 Ed Emberley;   113 Maxie Chambliss;   116 Steve Henry;   118 Doreen Gay-Kassel;   119–131 A. Delaney;   134–145 Arnold Lobel;   146 Diane Palmisciano;   147 Rick Brown;   148–149 Maxie Chambliss;   150–175 Steff Geissbuhler;   176–183 John Butler;   184–185 Steff Geissbuhler;   192–211 Denise and Fernando;   212–217 Catharine O'Neill;   218 (middle), 219, 220 (bottom), 221 (top), 226, 227, 229 Nancy Lee Walters;   218 (top & bottom), 220 (top), 222, 223 (bottom), 224 (top), 225, 228, 230, 231 Rosiland Solomon;   221 (bottom), 223 (top & middle), 224 (bottom) Jan Pyk

Photography   41 Jeffry W. Myers/The Stock Market;   43 Lawrence Migdale/Photo Researchers, Inc.;   77 Courtesy of Angela Johnson (top);   77 Courtesy of James Ransome (bottom);   113 Courtesy of Little, Brown and Company;   114–115 Superstock;   117 © C.K.Tsin 7/90;   132 Rod Williams/Bruce Coleman, Inc. (top);   132 Jeff Foott/Bruce Coleman, Inc. (bottom);   133 Norman Owen Tomalin/Bruce Coleman, Inc. (top);   133 *Animals Animals*/ © M. Austerman (bottom);   146 Adam Lobel/Reprinted courtesy of HarperCollins Children's Books;   187 *Animals Animals*/ © Jim Tutek;   188 David Frazier;   189 *Animals Animals*/ © Anthony Bannister (top);   189 Bernard Baudet/Superstock (bottom);   190 Michael P. Gadomski/Photo Researchers, Inc. (center left);   190 Leonard Lee Rue III/Photo Researchers, Inc. (center right);   190 *Animals Animals*/ © LLT Rhodes (top left);   190 K. Coppieters/Superstock (top right);   190 *Animals Animals*/ © Michael P. Gadomski (bottom left);   190 *Animals Animals*/ © Anthony Bannister (bottom right);   191 Bradley Smith/Photo Researchers, Inc. (center left);   191 Anthony Mercieca/Superstock (center right);   191 Arthus Bertrand/Photo Researchers, Inc. (top left);   191 *Animals Animals*/ © Margot Conte (top right);   191 Stev-olaf Lindblad/Photo Researchers, Inc. (bottom left);   191 Superstock (bottom right)

Assignment Photographers   76 Andrew Parsons (bottom);   213, 215, 217 David Shopper